Counting Your Body

Kristy Stark, M.A.Ed.

Publishing Credits

Rachelle Cracchiolo, M.S.Ed., *Publisher*
Conni Medina, M.A.Ed., *Managing Editor*
Nika Fabienke, Ed.D., *Series Developer*
June Kikuchi, *Content Director*
John Leach, *Assistant Editor*
Kevin Pham, *Graphic Designer*

TIME For Kids and the TIME For Kids logo are registered trademarks of TIME Inc. Used under license.

Image Credits: All images from iStock and/or Shutterstock.

Library of Congress Cataloging-in-Publication Data

Names: Stark, Kristy, author.
Title: Counting : your body / Kristy Stark, M.A.Ed.
Other titles: Your body
Description: Huntington Beach, CA : Teacher Created Materials, [2018] |
   Audience: Grades 4 to 6.
Identifiers: LCCN 2017042926 (print) | LCCN 2017048162 (ebook) | ISBN
   9781425853198 (eBook) | ISBN 9781425849450 (pbk.)
Subjects: LCSH: Animals--Juvenile literature. | Anatomy--Juvenile literature.
   | Veterinary anatomy--Juvenile literature. | Counting--Juvenile literature.
Classification: LCC QL49 (ebook) | LCC QL49 .S6754 2018 (print) | DDC
   590--dc23
LC record available at https://lccn.loc.gov/2017042926

Teacher Created Materials

5301 Oceanus Drive
Huntington Beach, CA 92649-1030
http://www.tcmpub.com

ISBN 978-1-4258-4945-0

© 2018 Teacher Created Materials, Inc.

Count the body parts.

I have one nose.

How about you?

I have one
tongue.

How about you?

I have two ears.

How about you?

I have ten
fingers.

How about you?

I have one
whole body.